DATE DUE			
6-30-00			
JUL 29 00			
APR 19 01			
11-27-01			
SEP 0 5			

5/00

**JACKSON
COUNTY**
Library Services

HEADQUARTERS
413 West Main Street
Medford, Oregon 97501

HIGH VOICE

SINGER'S CHRISTIAN WEDDING COLLECTION

ISBN 0-7935-9367-0

HAL•LEONARD®
CORPORATION
7777 W. BLUEMOUND RD. P.O. BOX 13819 MILWAUKEE, WI 53213

Visit Hal Leonard Online at
www.halleonard.com

SINGER'S CHRISTIAN WEDDING COLLECTION

Butterfly Kisses

Recorded by Bob Carlisle

Words and Music by RANDY THOMAS
and BOB CARLISLE

5

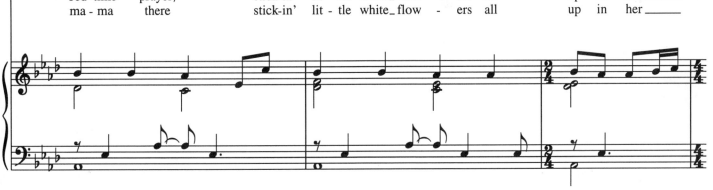

Cherish the Treasure

Recorded by Steve Green

Words and Music by
JON MOHR

15

Commitment Song

Recorded by Chris & Diane Machen

Words and Music by ROBERT STERLING
and CHRIS MACHEN

Moderately

O Lord,_ dear Lord, we come be-fore You now_ to
O Lord,_ dear Lord, let us nev-er turn_ a-way._ Let us

of-fer You_ a sac-ri-fice_ of praise._ And we pray, dear_ Lord, You'll
hon-or You_ and al-ways seek Your face._ And we pray, dear_ Lord, for-

bless our sol-emn vow_ that as long as we're_ to-geth-er_ the name of
give us when_ we stray._ Lead us back with ten-der mer-cy_ with Your

Flesh of My Flesh

Recorded by Leon Patillo

Words and Music by
LEON PATILLO

For Always
Recorded by BeBe & CeCe Winans

Words and Music by BEBE WINANS,
BILLY SPRAGUE and KEITH THOMAS

Go There with You

Recorded by Steven Curtis Chapman

Words and Music by
STEVEN CURTIS CHAPMAN

Love of the Lasting Kind

Words and Music by CLAIRE CLONINGER
and DON CASON

love, we'll stay in love, in per-fect love, in love of the last - ing kind.

God Causes All Things to Grow

Recorded by Steve Green

Words and Music by STEVEN CURTIS CHAPMAN
and STEVE GREEN

Household of Faith

Recorded by Steve & Marijean Green

Words by BRENT LAMB
Music by JOHN ROSASCO

With warmth (♩ = 66)

How Beautiful

Recorded by Twila Paris

Words and Music by
TWILA PARIS

56

I Could Never Promise You

Words and Music by
DON FRANCISCO

Slowly, with feeling

I could nev-er prom-ise _ you on just my strength a-lone, _

that all my life I'd care for _ you and love you as my own.

I've nev-er known the fu - ture, I on-ly see to-day; _

I Will Be Here
Recorded by Steven Curtis Chapman

Words and Music by
STEVEN CURTIS CHAPMAN

Lyrics under the staff:

To-mor-row morn-in' if you __ wake up and the sun does __ not __ ap-pear,

To-mor-row morn-in' if you __ wake up and the fu-ture is __ un-clear,

In This Very Room

Words and Music by RON and CAROL HARRIS

I.O.U. Me

Recorded by BeBe & CeCe Winans

Words and Music by BEBE WINANS, BILLY SPRAGUE,
KEITH THOMAS, THOMAS HEMBY and MIKE RAPP

Moderately, in 2

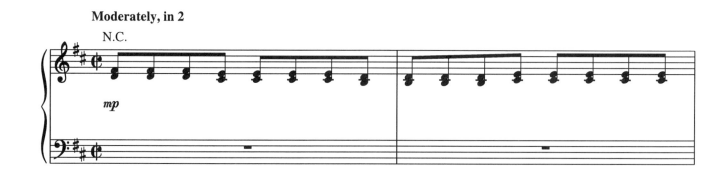

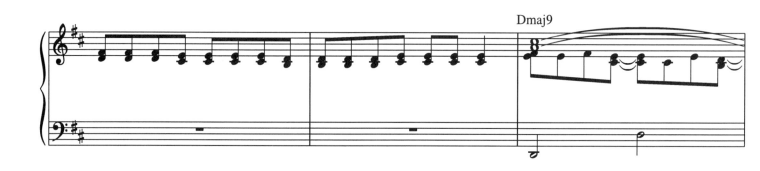

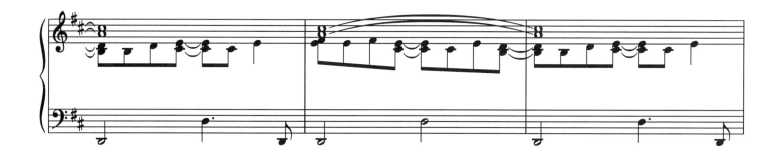

74

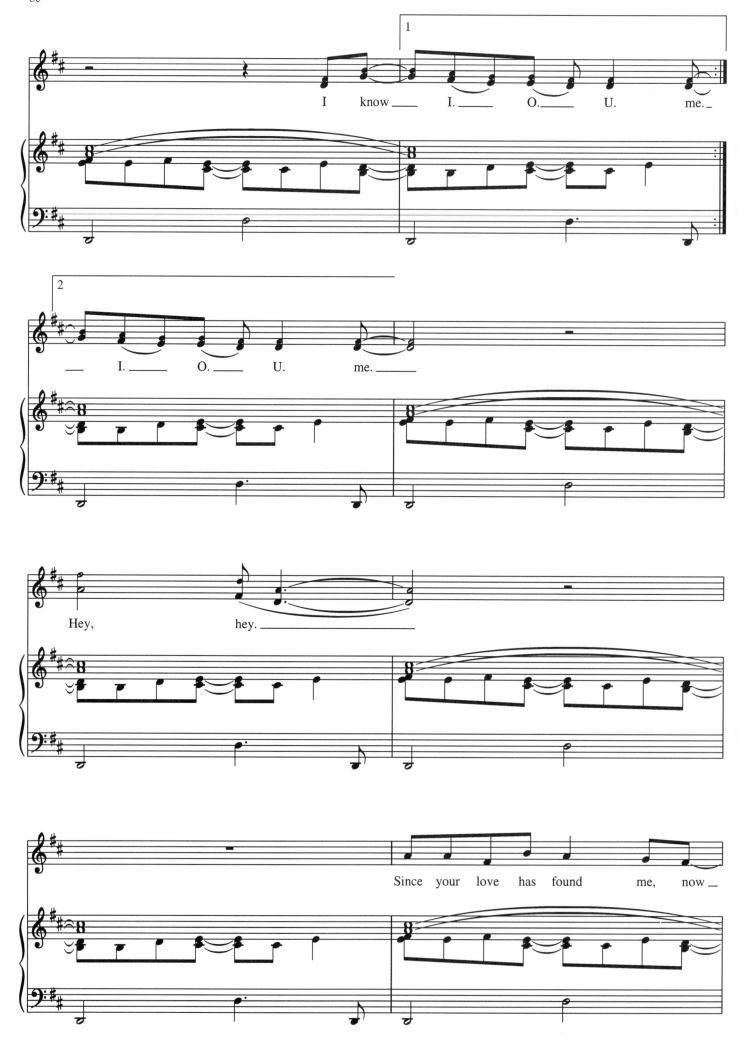

I'm liv-in' out your love. ___

Since your love has found me, now ___ I'm liv-in' out your love. ___

I know ___ I. ___ O. ___ U. me. ___

The Language of Jesus Is Love

Recorded by Scott Wesley Brown

Words and Music by PHILL McHUGH, GREG NELSON,
SCOTT WESLEY BROWN and PHIL NAISH

The Lord's Prayer

By ALBERT HAY MALOTTE

Poco meno mosso, e sonoramente

Lost Without You
Recorded by BeBe & CeCe Winans

Words and Music by BEBE WINANS
and KEITH THOMAS

Love Will Be Our Home

Recorded by Sandi Patty

Words and Music by
STEVEN CURTIS CHAPMAN

The ending either could be done loud or soft.

Only God Could Love You More

Words and Music by DWIGHT LILES
and NILES BOROP

Parent's Prayer
(Let Go of Two)
Recorded by Steven Curtis Chapman

Words and Music by
GREG DAVIS

Song of Reconciliation

Recorded by Susan Ashton, Margaret Becker & Christine Denté

Words and Music by
WAYNE KIRKPATRICK

Perfect Union

Words and Music by JOHN ANDREW SCHREINER
and MATTHEW WARD

Portrait of Love

Recorded by John Byron

Words and Music by KENNY WOOD
and BILLY CROCKETT

120

Seekers of Your Heart

Recorded by Larnelle Harris

Words and Music by MELODIE TUNNEY,
DICK TUNNEY and BEVERLY DARNALL

This Is the Day
(A Wedding Song)

Words and Music by
SCOTT WESLEY BROWN

Moderately fast, flowing

This is the day __ that the Lord __ hath __ made, __ and
This is the love __ that the Lord __ hath __ made; __ that

I'm so glad __ He made you. __ With
you and __ I, __ we are one. __ With

each ris - in' sun you are here by my side, you are
Love's mys - ter - y is un - fold - ing to - day,

this is the day, _

this is the day. _

rit.

This Very Day

Recorded by Paul Overstreet

Words and Music by JOHN ELLIOTT
and PAUL OVERSTREET

I've been search-ing all __ my life __ for the wom-an I __ was meant __ to make __ my __ wife. And

Like the an-swer to __ my prayers, __ from this day on __ I'll wake __ to find __ her __ there. And

The Wedding

Recorded by Michael Card

Words and Music by
MICHAEL CARD

Lord ___ of Light, oh come to this wed-ding; ___ take ___ the doubt and dark-ness a - way.

136

CODA

Time for Joy

Recorded by Lawrence Craig Shackley

Words and Music by
GERRY LIMPIC

Moderately slow, with expression

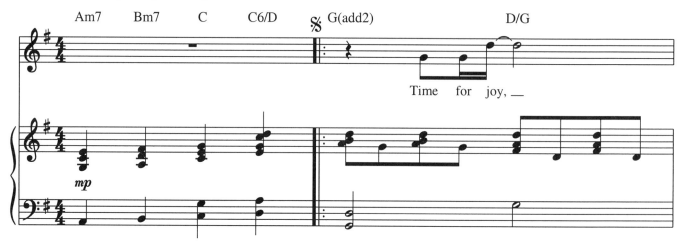

Time for joy, __

time __ for cheer, that is __ why we all _____ are here. __

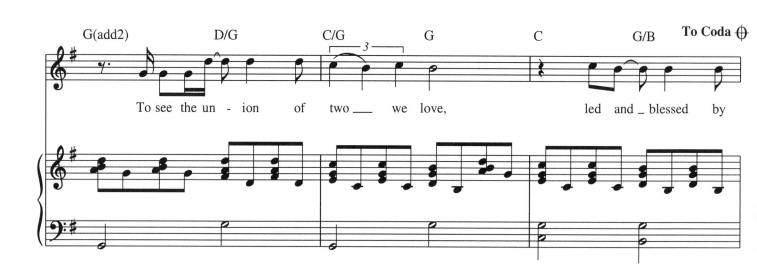

To see the un - ion of two __ we love, led and _ blessed by

Wedding Prayer

Words and Music by
MARY RICE HOPKINS

Where There Is Love

Recorded by Scott Wesley Brown

Words and Music by PHILL McHUGH
and GREG NELSON

Wedding COLLECTIONS FOR VOICE
From Hal Leonard

THE SINGER'S WEDDING ANTHOLOGY

An unprecedented, comprehensive look at wedding repertoire. Rather than just one style of music, like most wedding collections for voice, we have included classical and traditional material, popular songs, and contemporary Christian music. The anthology is available in 3 versions: High Voice, Low Voice, and Duets. The two solo volumes (High and Low) contain the same 45 selections, but in appropriate keys to high or low voices. Includes: I Swear • Just the Way You Are • When I Fall in Love • Someone Like You • The Language of Jesus Is Love • God Causes All Things to Grow • I Will Be Here • Ave Maria • Bist Du Bei Mir • Entreat Me Not to Leave Thee • Panis Angelicus • Whither Thou Goest • and many others. The duet collection contains 25 songs, including: Up Where We Belong • All I Ask of You • Endless Love • Let It Be Me • Household of Faith • Jesu Joy of Man's Desiring • Panis Angelicus • and many others.

00740006	High Voice	$19.95
00740008	Low Voice	$19.95
00740005	Duets	$14.95

WEDDING CLASSICS

The definitive collection of 12 classical and traditional favorites for the wedding service, packaged with an excellent recording of full performances (featuring top quality young singers) and accompaniments only. Contents: Bist du Bei Mir (Bach) • Entreat Me Not to Leave Thee (Gounod) • Because, Wher'er You Walk (Handel) • Oh Promise Me, Ich Liebe Dich (Grieg) • Ave Maria (Schubert) • Ave Maria (Bach/Gounod) • Du Ring An Meinem Finger (Schumann) • Widmung (Schumann) • I Love You Truly, Pur Ti Miro (Monteverdi – duet).

00740053 High Voice Book/CD package. *$17.95*
00740054 Low Voice Book/CD package *$17.95*

10 POPULAR WEDDING DUETS
with a companion CD

10 duets for the wedding. The companion CD contains two performances of each song, one with singers, the other is the orchestrated instrumental track for accompaniment. Contents: All I Ask of You • Annie's Song • Don't Know Much • Endless Love • I Swear • In My Life • Let It Be Me • True Love • Up Where We Belong • When I Fall in Love.

00740002 Book/CD package. *$19.95*

10 WEDDING SOLOS
with a companion CD

A terrific, useful collection of 10 songs for the wedding, including both popular songs and contemporary Christian material. There are two versions of each song on the companion CD, first with full performances with singers, then with the instrumental accompaniments only. Contents: Here, There and Everywhere • I Swear • The Promise • Someone Like You • Starting Here Starting Now • God Causes All Things to Grow • Parent's Prayer • This Is the Day • Wedding Prayer • Where There Is Love.

00740004 High Voice Book/CD package *$19.95*
00740009 Low Voice Book/CD package. *$19.95*

12 WEDDING SONGS
arranged for medium voice and fingerstyle guitar

A practical collection of music chosen particularly for the wedding, in new arrangements designed to flatter voice with guitar accompaniment. The collection combines classical/traditional and popular selections. The guitar part is presented in both standard notation and tablature. Contents: Annie's Song • Ave Maria (Schubert) • The First Time Ever I Saw Your Face • Here, There and Everywhere • I Swear • If • In My Life • Jesu, Joy of Man's Desiring • Let It Be Me • Unchained Melody • When I Fall in Love • You Needed Me.

00740007 . . . . *$12.95*

SINGER'S CHRISTIAN WEDDING COLLECTION

30 songs, including: Butterfly Kisses • Cherish the Treasure • Commitment Song • Household of Faith • How Beautiful • I Will Be Here • Lost Without You • Love Will Be Our Home • Parent's Prayer (Let Go of Two) • This Is the Day (A Wedding Song) • and more.

| 00740108 | High Voice | $19.95 |
| 00740109 | Low Voice | $19.95 |

FOR MORE INFORMATION, SEE YOUR LOCAL MUSIC DEALER,
OR WRITE TO:

HAL•LEONARD® CORPORATION

7777 W. BLUEMOUND RD. P.O. BOX 13819 MILWAUKEE, WI 53213

Prices, contents and availability subject to change without notice. Some products may not be available outside the U.S.A.